Paradise Flowers.

The Ultimate Book of Patchwork Flora.

By Angela Madden.

Acknowledgements.
Grateful thanks are due to Tom Finniear of Flame Ltd. Kings Langley Herts.
(Apple Authorised Service Provider) ... who answered my anguished distress
call when my computer was not cooperating and without whom this book would
not have been completed ....

Also to Vycombe Arts. Fen Way, Fen Walk. Woodbridge Suffolk. P12 4AS for
letting me try out different fabric paints. (They offer a fast Mail order service.)

Lastly also to Mr. Akira Sawai of Clover MFG. Co. Ltd. Osaka. Japan. for
enabling me to use their wonderful 'Quick Bias^{TM}'tape in several of the projects
shown in this book.

In addition special thanks are due to the following ...

Sue Martin, Jane Plowman, and Martin Mc Donald for technical assistance.

Barbara Corbett, Nora Field, Jenny Hipperson, Alison King, Sue Martin,
Michelle Maloney, Kathleen McMahon, Jane Plowman, Mary Rich, Shirley
Winchester, and Judy Wilson, who agreed to be my 'guinea pigs' and following
a workshop, kindly lent their work to be photographed

'Paradise Flowers' © 1996 Angela Madden.

ISBN 0 952 1060 5 1.
First edition 1998.

M.C.Q. Publications.	Distributor in U.S.A.	Distributor in New Zealand.
19, Barlings Rd.	Quilters' Resource Inc.	Margaret Barrett Distributors.
Harpenden. Herts.	P.O. Box 148850.	19, Beasley Ave.
AL5 2AL.	Chicago. Illinois 60614.	P.O. Box 12 - 034.
England.	312 - 278 - 5795.	Penrose. Auckland.

Index

Page.

Introduction

Flowers and quilts are a truly magical combination. From the earliest days of patchwork, floral images have been lovingly reproduced in fabric. Generally these flowers have followed two quite separate needlework paths ....
geometric representations and realistic images. The former mainly appeared in pieced patchwork patterns and the latter in appliqué designs.

This book takes the patchwork route. Designs can be geometric or, if you prefer they can be created with a softer, more realistic look. Instructions for piecing cover both styles or a combination. These flowers can also be worked very effectively using other techniques, such as quilting, fabric embellishment, stencilling, stained glass and trapunto, These instructions are also included. Several techniques can also be combined within the same item.

Have you ever imagined how much fun it would be to become a Mother Nature figure recreating a 'Paradise garden' in patchwork terms ... to be able to dream up a flower ... plain or fancy .... in any petal shape or colour ..... and make it appear? To have the ability to think of new plant formations and leaves, as well as including your present favourites ... combining them in any way you choose?

Well ..... now you can experience that fun. You can design fabric flowers to suit every purpose, speedily and easily. First time sewers and experienced patchworkers alike can assemble these blooms efficiently and accurately ......
a vital prerequisite in the process of having fun !! ....
because if sewing is not fun..... why are we sewing?

Paradise Flowers are easily drafted, requiring no special artistic expertise for success. They can be used in a variety of ways to create quilts of any size, depending on the level of commitment and time ...... from a single block cushion to a multi-block, king size quilt. Any item can be easily assembled using basic sewing skills.

Designs can contain a simple lone flower, or combine many flowers in amazing pattern formations that rival anything a professional designer can achieve with the aid of a hi - tech computer. These are the kinds of quilts that are admired at quilt shows .... and win the prizes!

Whatever you do with these techniques, I hope that they bring you much pleasure and satisfaction and enable you to create quilts that you love.

Here are some general points to make life easier while you are sewing Paradise Flowers

1. Freezer paper is an essential aid to the techniques in this book. .... If you are unfamiliar with this type of paper ... it is useful because it sticks to fabric when ironed, shiny side down .... but is easily removed, leaving no residue.

It therefore makes great templates. Designs are drafted on the dull side.

It is available by the roll in U.S.A. as a food wrap and also from most quilt shops.

It is used as the outer wrappers for many... **but not all** ... packets of photocopying paper. Check that yours sticks to fabric before starting to design. These wrappers can be a little stiff and usually carry printing, so felt pen may be needed to clarify your design lines. The wrapper size is more limiting than purchased rolls ...

and be sure to remove the glue, or it will damage your fabric.

I have recently discovered a great new free source ..... it is used as packing between some brands of new aluminium printing plates, so it is well worth requesting local printing firms to save it for you. Printers will not call it 'freezer paper', so a description of the dull and shiny side will probably be necessary. These sheets are blank and are usually wider than supermarket paper on the roll.

2. Spray starch all fabric before starting work ... making it easier to handle, especially washed or hand dyed fabric which has lost its 'crispness.' Starch will add stiffness for just as long as it is required. Handling swiftly restores softness and drape. Pieced designs also benefit from a light starching before quilting.

Iron on the wrong side, as over- enthusiasm may cause fabric to become shiny.

3. Use long, thin pins.   They make such a difference when aligning fabric pieces for sewing .... I personally like the type with the flat 'daisy' shaped heads.

4. Iron seams as you work ... keep your ironing board near at all times.

This makes a great difference to the degree of accuracy achieved. The extra effort is worthwhile, as you will probably be looking at the finished result for a long time. One good quality item is worth several roughly matched ones, pieced in the same amount of time. I keep a small ironing board and travelling iron on the table beside me as I work. This is more convenient than having to keep going to the full sized board. (Although I would probably benefit from the exercise !)

The practice of peeling off the freezer paper shapes and re-ironing them over the seam allowance, as described in the text, is an **<u>essential</u>** aid to accuracy.

5. Stock up on size 60 machine needles.   They have thin shanks so make small holes. They do a great job on the curved seam technique described. However, they are inclined to break easily, so are not recommended for utility sewing.

6. If you are joining pieces of freezer paper for larger projects ... use clear sticky tape on the dull side of the paper. Some tape can be written upon (Magic Tape)^{TM} Test that your brand will not melt when ironed. The iron temperature is a crucial factor.

7. Fusi - Knit^{TM} is used in some of the following techniques ... e.g. 'Stained glass'
It is a 'see through' nylon interfacing which can be heat fused, using an iron, to the wrong side of fabric or patchwork. This can add stability to a piece of work or make stained glass projects easier and faster to complete.

Many quilt shops now stock Fusi - knit^{TM} alongside their fabric range. Technically it is a dress making interfacing so is also available from a wide range of fabric shops. It is sold by the metre at approx 20ins. wide, in black, white, ivory and grey, to suit both light and dark projects.

Fusi - knit^{TM} also benefits wearable patchwork projects where wadding would add too much bulk. Each pieced section should be completed separately. Apply the fusible to the wrong side over the pieced seams before making up. Garments will gain body and stability, appearing smoother without becoming stiff.
Once an interfacing has been fused to a fabric it will always feel firmer, but unlike many fusibles, Fusi - knit^{TM} does not make the fabric hard and rigid. It still allows a good degree of drape. Being a knit interfacing there is some stretch in the width wise direction.

Test fuse a sample ..... to check the temperature at which your iron achieves the most satisfactory permanent bond.

1. Cut matching pieces of fabric and Fusi - knit^{TM} ..... e.g. 6 x 6 ins.

2. Place the coated side of the fusible face down, on the wrong side of your fabric.

3. Cover with a lightweight pressing cloth.

4. Press, on a 'wool' setting for 10 - 12 seconds which is the minimum time necessary to fuse. Alter the heat setting if necessary. The manufacturer's instructions suggest steam pressing, but I use a dry iron as this makes the fabric less stiff. The bond produced is still sufficient for my purposes.... try both methods, then feel the difference before deciding your own preference.

5. Press fabric again on the right side to aid smooth bonding.

6. Allow to become cold before handling.

If you have pressed the fusible or fabric incorrectly.......
they can be separated before they cool.
If they have already become cold ... warm them by lightly ironing once again.

Lastly......

8. Please note that the freezer paper piecing technique described in this book will reverse the drafted design. This is pointed out for information only. The technique described allows for a choice of design direction.

Planting The Seed ......Planning The Design

Paradise Flowers are surprisingly easy to design. They need no special aptitudes, artistic skill, or tools ..... just a little 'know - how' and some practice which will give you confidence to explore the limitless possibilities.

You will need...

- Scrap paper for practice designs and master copies.
- Freezer paper for duplicate copies..... *i.e. those destined to be sewn,*
- Mechanical pencils are good drafting tools as they always draw fine, accurate lines.
- A soft eraser.
- A ruler... I prefer those with a printed grid, which is great for checking corners are square, as well as drafting lines.
(Transparent rotary cutting rulers, both long and short are ideal.)
 Curved lines can easily be drafted by the 'non - technical' method ....
around plates, saucers, glasses, cups and saucepans, or trays if you need big ones .... check out the kitchen 'technical drafting' cupboards !!
- Some thin cardboard ... cereal packets are fine.

Start by designing a square block containing a centrally placed flower.

1.   Draw a square which is the same size as the intended finished block ..... excluding seam allowances ...   (6 ins. is recommended for practice designs.)

2. For practice designs mark all the sides of the square at 1 in. intervals.

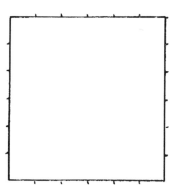

Tip.....
Always choose easy measurements for block sides,
i.e. complete, or half inches.... so that marked intervals are all the same size.
Blocks are then easily joined together to form linking patterns,
and sizes can be speedily doubled or halved.
This eliminates any tricky mathematical calculations which might result
when block sides contain awkward fractions of an inch.

The side interval can be altered to suit any block size. In theory it can be any measurement ..... you are the designer................ so you can choose !.......
(However, I use 1in. most of the time.)

3. Number the interval marks as follows, Mark all four corners as number 1

4. Continue numbering along the sides in sequence...
across the top ...... left to right.
across the base .... left to right.
and down each side.

5. The practice design will contain a flower centrally placed, north to south within the square. It will be positioned between the mid point on the top ....
and the mid point on the base.

6. In sides containing an even number of marks there will already be a number at the mid point.

In odd numbered sides the mid point of the top and base will require an extra mark to be added between numbers.

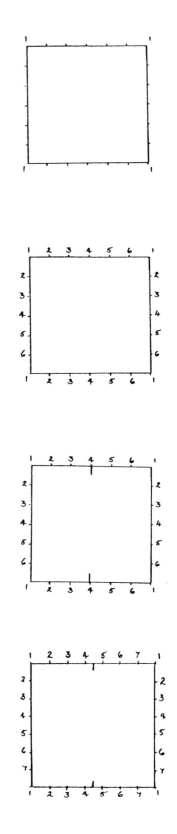

7. Join top and base centre marks
with a straight line......
this will form the central flower stalk.

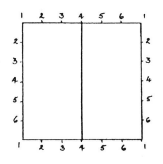

8. We will draft this first practice design with leaves placed symmetrically on either side of the central stalk. (Later designs can be asymmetrical if you wish)

Link base (B) mark 4 to both side marks 2
with straight lines. These lines will
form the central vein of each side leaf.

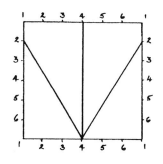

9. Now that you can see the skeleton
of the plant, it becomes possible to judge
the size of the flower head in relation
to the rest.

The flower head will be placed at the top
of the central stalk on this occasion...

Align your ruler with both side numbers 3.
and mark the stalk where the ruler crosses A.
The flower head will be positioned
above this mark.

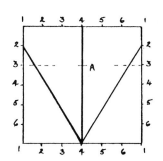

10. To draft a simple side view flower
head ....
join A to both top (T) 2 and 6.

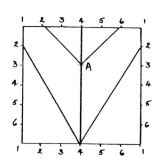

11. The square contains identical right and left halves.

Align your ruler with T4 and right (R) 5.

Draw the line within the flower head...
ending at B.

Repeat with T 4 and left (L) 5.
This completes one central petal.

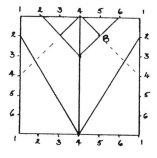

12. Align ruler with T2 and R3 ....
draw a line from T2
to the top of the central petal..... C.

Repeat from T6 to L3 ... completing both
side petals of this simple flower head.

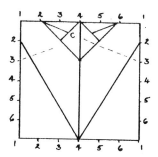

13. Drafting leaves always begins with a single
line. This may link numbers on any two sides
of the block, or begin on the flower stalk.

Sometimes this line will form the central
vein of the leaf.

Sometimes it may form a stalk
to which several leaves can be attached.
These leaves may point in opposite directions.

Sometimes it will form the side edge of a leaf.

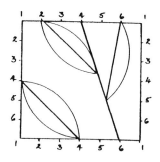

14. Continue the practice design
by adding curved sides to the leaf ....
Use a plate or saucer for this.
(Experiment with different size plates
and saucers to find one which reaches
between the two points and gives a nice curve.)

Place the curved edge so that it touches
both R 2 and B 4, enabling you to draft a
suitable curve connecting them,
on the top of the vein line.

Repeat from L2 to B4.
This forms the upper half of both leaves.

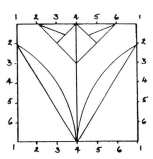

10

15. To complete each leaf ....
Use a curve once again to draft the other half.
It can be a different size if you wish.

First align your ruler with both side marks 6.
Mark level 6 on the flower stem ... D..

This time we will use only a part of the vein line.

Align the edge of the curve with R2 and D
drawing the curve on the underside of the leaf,
stopping at the vein line.
Repeat from L2.

16. The last move in this practice design is to
add the other side of the flower stalk.
Offset this to either the right or the left side
of the central stalk.

Draft this line parallel to the stalk line, ...
at approx 1/4 in. distance ...
from the flower head to the leaf.

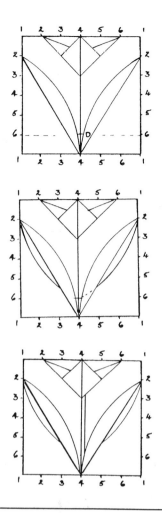

Tip...

**Offsetting the stalk to one side makes
the assembly of the block much easier
in designs where a central upright
flower head joins the stalk with a point.**

**The same is also true at the base of a stalk ...
where a central stalk meets leaves with
a point.**

**When assembling the block, the stalk
will become part of the background on
the side to which it has been offset.**

**This facilitates the easy completion
of the block by joining the central seam**

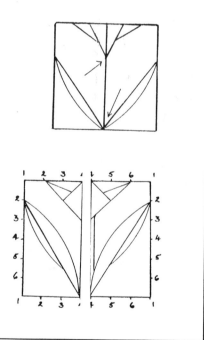

This slight asymmetry will not detract
from the finished design...... in fact most
people will never notice it at all !

Design Tips

Once you have completed your first practice design try a few more. Follow the main principles, but be a little creative in their application. Mixing curves with straight lines will always enhance and soften flower and leaf shapes.
The techniques described later ensure that curved seams will be easy to sew.

Your imagination is the only limitation ....   as you consider the following ....

1. Flower heads can take many different shapes; all are easy to draft.

2. Flowers can be viewed from different directions.................
This will inevitably change their shape.

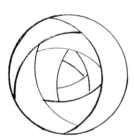

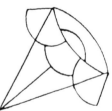

Face on.   **Side.**   **Side tilted.**

3. Several flowers can be included
in the same block.
If they are symmetrical,
and very closely related
in size and shape,
the block will appear
stylised and traditional.

If they are asymmetrical
and varied, the effect will be
more natural and quirky.

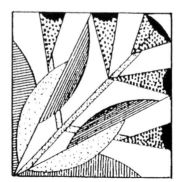

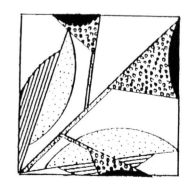

4. Blocks containing flowers or leaves only can also be drafted ....
these can be useful as connecting blocks.

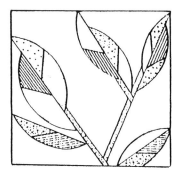

They can also be used to create vines, and borders, and ....
for lengthening the stalks of flowers

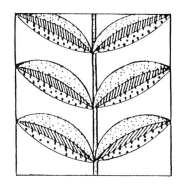

5. Curves do not have to be added to both sides of the central vein when drafting leaves.

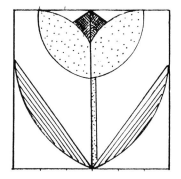

A curve on one side may be quite sufficient......

The curves can match .... or not, on either side of the central vein ... you choose.

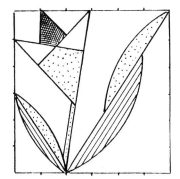

Leaves can also be made up entirely of curved lines.

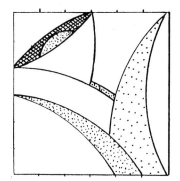

6. Leaves can be drafted using straight lines only............
e.g. join B5 to R2 and B3 to L2.

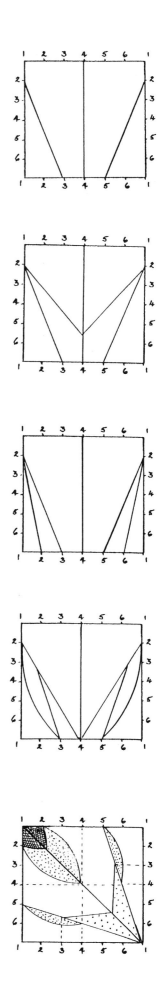

Lines can be added above the central vein to complete the leaf,
e.g. from the flower stalk to R2.

The starting position on the flower stalk can be a random choice to suit the design .....
because it will be easy to draft the corresponding line to L2 from exactly the same point, as it is the mirror image.

Alternatively, lines can be added below the flower stalk ....
e.g. from B2 to L2 and B6 to R 2.

Leaves can also be drafted from combinations of straight and curved lines.

7. Design lines ending on the side of a block should always end on a numbered mark.

Within a block they can begin and end anywhere you choose ...
provided ....
that if you needed to reproduce a line accurately for symmetry, or for 'cloning' a block, the *identical* beginning and end positions can be identified.

14

8. After drafting the central leaf vein, you may choose to use only part of it for the leaf.

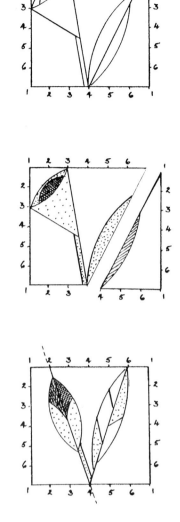

It is necessary, however, to leave the left-over portion of line in place ...... where it crosses the background space.

This extra portion of line will be used as a construction seam to ease the final assembly of the block.

This seam will not look unsightly .... and can be completely disguised with a quilting pattern if you wish.

9. Lines may also be drafted beyond the tips of flowers or buds .... and can be treated in the same way,

Tip.
While you are drafting designs, always check that you are not creating flowers or leaves which do not link either with an outside edge ... or another seam line. These would be impossible to assemble without having to change direction abruptly mid seam ... a tricky sewing task.

Such 'free floating' parts of a design can only be included efficiently if they are appliqued on to the background.

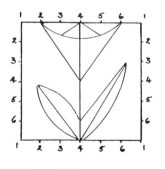

10. Side interval marks are useful ......

a. as registration points for beginning and ending the lines which create flowers and leaves.

b. to ensure both sides of the block look the same in symmetrical blocks

c. as linking points for patterns in adjoining blocks .....
when each block forms a single unit within a larger multi - block design.

Where links are formed between leaves and flowers in adjoining blocks, harmonious composite patterns result.

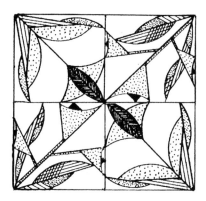

Such patterns will be satisfying and pleasing to the eye.

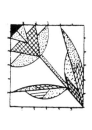

Do not worry unduly about links, you will find that they often take care of themselves, in multiples of the same design.
It is not necessary to create links between *every* flower and leaf. But if *all* flowers and leaves are free floating and disconnected the resulting patterns may appear 'busy' and disordered. This is more likely to happen when mixing blocks containing different patterns.
In this instance you will need to alter the designs, making flowers and leaves start from the same side number in neighbouring blocks.

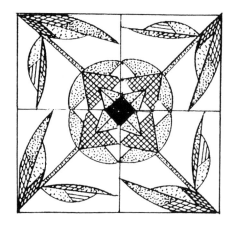

Of course side links do not matter at all if a block is to stand alone.

d. They enable the reproduction of blocks in a different size.

e.g. Half, quarter, or double size blocks are easily re - drafted using a different interval between marks.
To enlarge your 6 in. practice block to 12 in. draw a 12 in. square with intervals at 2 in. on all sides. Draw lines joining the same interval marks as on the original block.

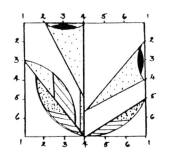

16

Cloisonne Style Lilies.

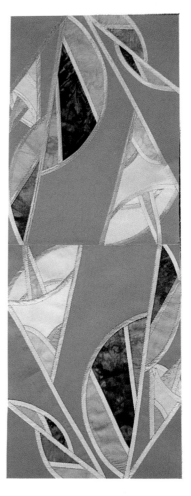

Playing with pattern options.

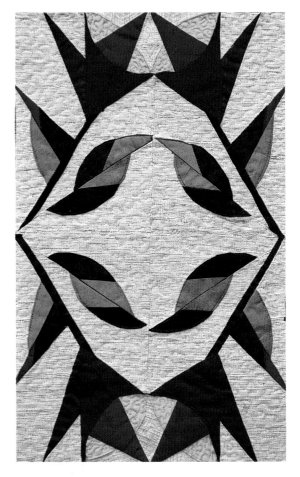

**Centre detail...
(another four block pattern option.)**

'Hoards of Hemerocallis' by Barbara Corbett.

Redbourne. Herts.   **Wallhanging 36ins. x 14 1/2 ins.**

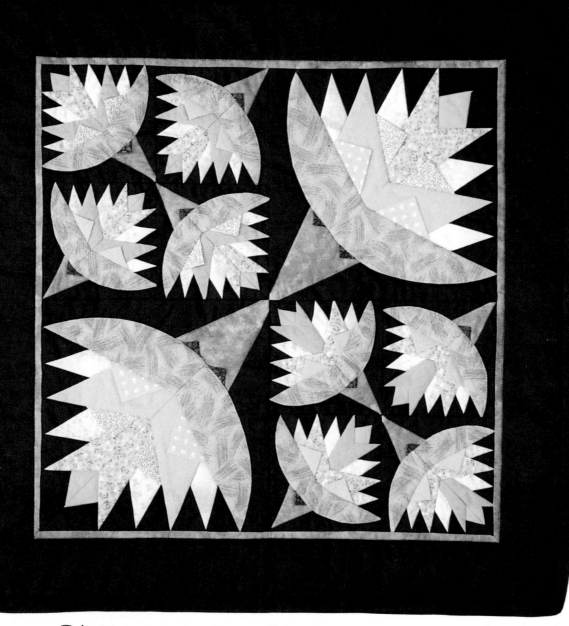

Wallhanging by Jane Plowman. **Boxmoor. Herts.**
22ins. x 22ins.

**Contains half size blocks
and 'Prarie point' inserts.**

Wallhanging by Nora Field.
Boxmoor. Herts.
36ins. x 22ins.

Contains bead embellishment.

Wallhanging by Sue Martin.
Boxmoor. Herts
31ins. x 31ins.

'Quintet' by Sue Martin.

'First Flowers' by Shirley Winchester.
Harpenden. Herts.

'Bobbydazzeler'
by Jenny Hipperson.
Harpenden. Herts.
38ins.x 38ins.

Wallhanging by Sue Martin.
31ins. x 31ins.
Using half size blocks.

Detail.

'Golden Splendor.'
by the author.
40ins.x 16 1/2ins.

'I've got the Blues' by Sue Martin.

Eight slice design. 28 1/2 ins. x 28 1/2ins

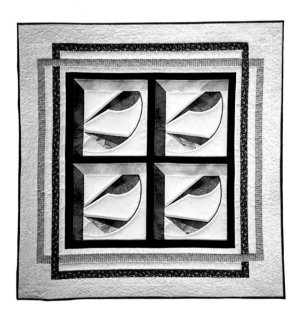

'Ikebana' 33ins. x 33ins.

Small wallhanging. **25ins. x 25ins.**
**Note how the rectangle blocks in the border
create a circular floral design.
Hand quilted.**

Planting Flowers Within a Block

Flower stalks can be placed in different positions within any block. This greatly increases the design possibilities. All alternatives are just as simple to draft as the centrally placed stalk.

The basic principles are always the same.

The various stalk placement options are....

1. A central stalk with symmetrically placed leaves .... creates matching half designs.

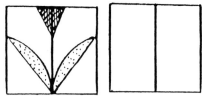

2. A central stalk with asymmetrically placed leaves. Design halves do not match.

3. A diagonally placed stalk ... with symmetrically placed leaves. Design halves match.

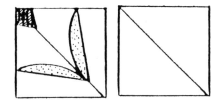

4. A diagonally placed stalk ... with asymmetrically placed leaves. Design halves do not match.

5. An off centre stalk... Asymmetrical only. Halves do not match.

6. Multiple flowers... Symmetrical. Halves match.

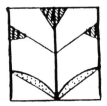

7. Multiple flowers.... Asymmetrical. Halves do not match.

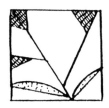

A single flower unit can look great if used on its own ....
or amazing if combined with others in a more complicated pattern formation.
This is where a little time playing with symmetry can be both fun and valuable.

Even if you have never, ever, designed anything in your life before ....
you can easily create an endless supply of beautiful, varied, original designs.

'Symmetry' is defined in the Oxford Dictionary as......
'Beauty resulting from the right proportion of parts' ... or ....
'divisibility into two or more parts, each of the same shape'

Using blocks in different symmetrical pattern configurations can produce markedly different end results. Arranging paper designs will enable you to discover really outstanding block combinations.
This is really a fun activity ... **and it makes sense to find the best block combinations .... before you spend time sewing them together !!!**

Draft a flower block... (or better still draft several different blocks.) Use mirrors, either aligned along one side of a block or, hinged together and placed along two sides, at the corner of a design. Even better ... take block designs to a photocopy shop .... reduce them in size .... duplicate 8 or 16 copies.... add colour ... then play.

This can be a therapeutic and relaxing way to open up creative potential you never knew existed.
Everyone has this potential ... even if your school art lessons only taught you that 'you can't draw'. This kind of designing has nothing whatever to do with drawing ... it's just making straight and curved lines using a ruler or plate.

I have never met anyone, of any age, who couldn't create beautiful original designs if they were shown the easy way ...
provided that they were open minded enough to give it a try.
The choice is yours ... stick with the safe, but dull route .... always copy other people's designs .... or ... live dangerously ... have a go ... branch out and bloom!
If you do .... you will never go back to copying.

Quilt blocks, traditional or otherwise ... are not all equally worthy of spending time on. You will be amazed at the different pattern possibilities that occur from combining multiples of one block .... impossible to visualise just by looking at it in isolation.

Once I have created a new block I am fascinated by the idea that all these variations exist ... just waiting for me to discover the one that I like best.

So imagine the many more intriguing possibilities which result from combining two or more different blocks.

1. The easiest way to become familiar with these possibilities is by examining our practice square containing the central flower with symmetrically placed leaves ....

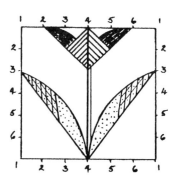

The block has four sides ... all are different.

Opposite sides look similar ... but are reversed.

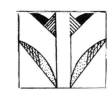

Any side can be butted up to any of the four sides of another identical block.

Different pattern links will result. You may like some more than others.

2. Blocks which are joined edge to edge in an orderly sequence produce predictable patterns.

The type of pattern depends entirely on which edges are repeatedly joined up.

3. When two (or more) units are linked they can be considered to have formed a new unique pattern unit.

4. Placing the flower in different positions within the block will once again increase the number of patterns possible when blocks are combined .....
and imagine the endless variations created by joining blocks containing different flowers ... wow!

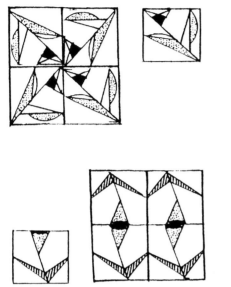

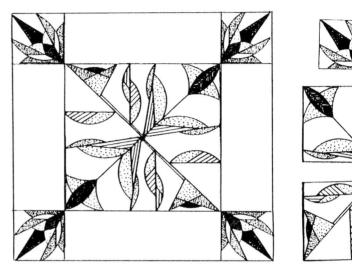

5. However ... there is something else to consider ....

some blocks are **symmetrical** ...
and some are **asymmetrical.**

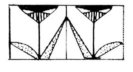

6. All asymmetrical designs .....
and **diagonally placed** symmetrical ones...
can be flipped ..... *in any direction* ...
to produce a reverse or mirror image.

This is called 'reflection'.

7. Symmetrical designs ....
with a **north/south division** ...
behave differently .....
flipping them sideways will produce
a reflection identical to the original.
They must be flipped top over bottom
to create a different reverse pattern.

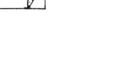

8. Flipped blocks always produce new
symmetrical patterns .... regardless of
whether the individual blocks are
symmetrical or asymmetrical.

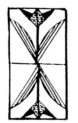

A Whole Garden From Just One Block

A flower on its own is lovely .... but massed impact can stop you in your tracks.
Our grandmothers created many patterns from simple blocks such as 'log cabin' ...
now look what you can do with one of your own original blocks!

There are at least **eighteen different ways** of using the same
asymmetrical block, with a north / south positioned stalk,
in groups of four.... flipping and / or rotating the original
block.

A group of four could be used for a cushion, wall hanging
or medallion... or ... joining further blocks produces a
completely new all over quilt design.
All are well worth exploring, producing completely
different medallion and sheet patterns.........

1.

2.

3.

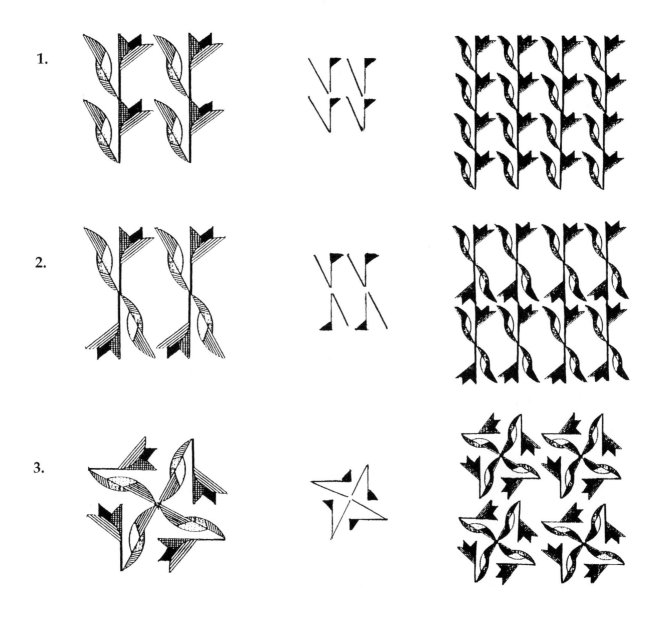

29

4.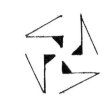

5.

6.

7.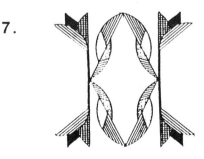

8.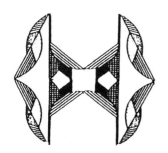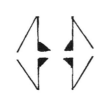

9.

10.

11.

12.

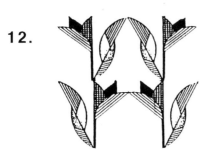  

13.

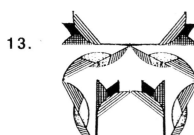  

14

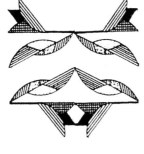 

15.

16.

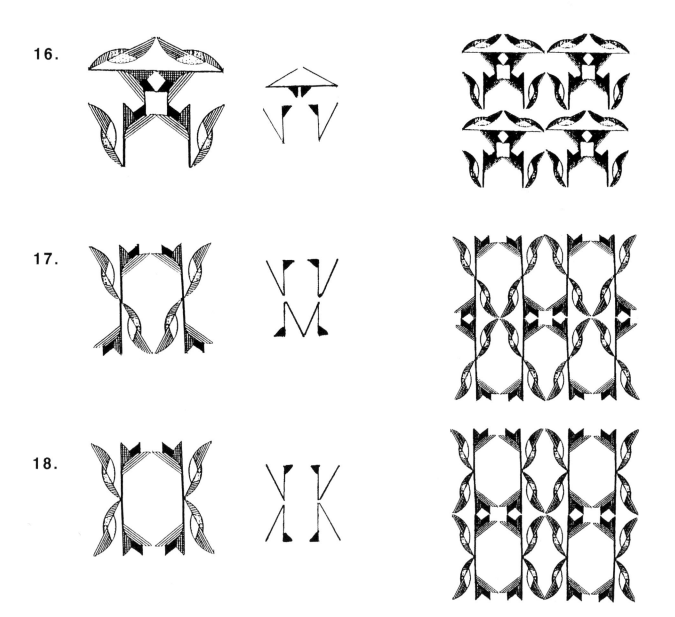

17.

18.

Using alternatives 13 ..... 16 ... and 17..... as flipped pairs ..... creates more new medallion designs.

Delightful Diagonals

1. Any block containing a diagonal design ....
when turned through 90 degrees ..... i.e. rotated...
then combined in groups of four,
will create **four** different patterns ......
when matching corners are repeatedly
placed at the design centre.

A   B

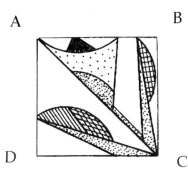

D   C

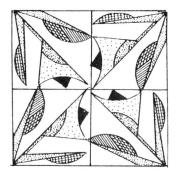

Corner A in centre.

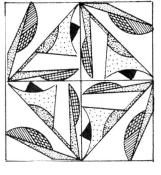

Corner B in centre.

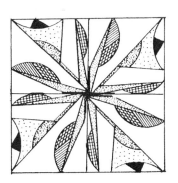

Corner C in centre.

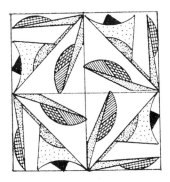

Corner D in centre

When playing with paper blocks ... mark the corners A.B.C.D. ...
Place all the A's together, then the B's etc. to identify the variation you prefer.

2. If any one of these new four block combinations is linked with another three of the same .... four more patterns develop .....

A.

B.

C.

D.

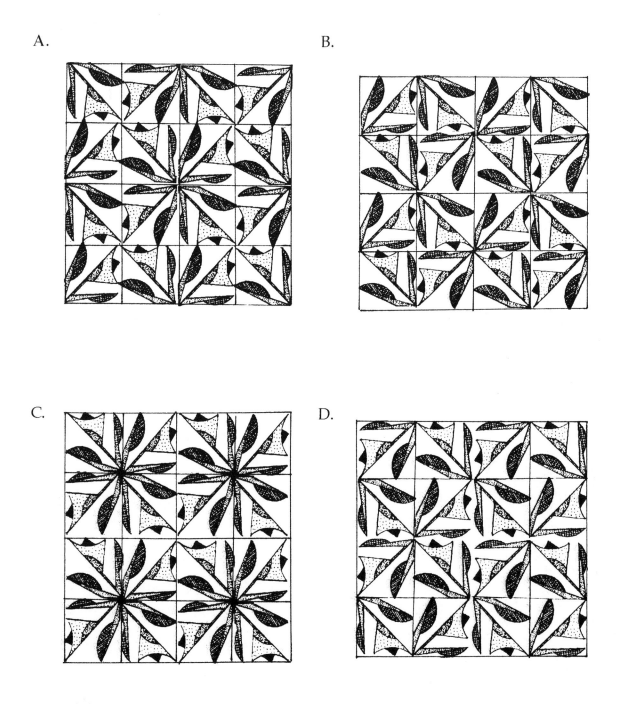

Any of these 16 block variations would make a great quilt ....
and it is completely original to you.

If you look closely at these block variations, you will see that the centre four blocks of each one are actually one of the other block combinations.
e.g. The centre of block A four times design .... is block C !

3. These 16 block designs are really created from two related 4 block patterns ....
so if more of the same are joined ...... only two sheet patterns will result.

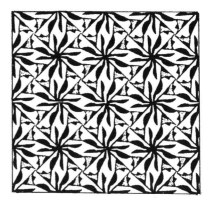

Two patterns will be found in one of the sheet designs ....
and the remaining two in the other.

↑   ↑

    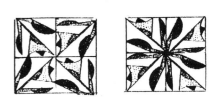

4. Many further pattern possibilities are created when the four block designs are joined in different combinations.

5. If 2 of the original 4 blocks are flipped along each of its sides in turn .... and mirrored pairs are joined .... **four new patterns are created.**

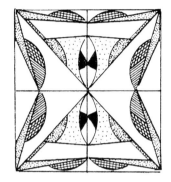

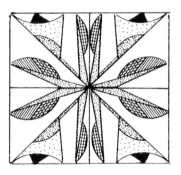
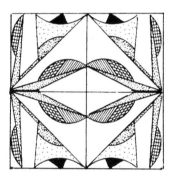

6. and also new 16 block designs ....

.... in which you can identify all four individual 4 block designs ..... combined in different positions.

7. This time the four designs will produce only one sheet pattern which contains them all.

8. Since all 4 block combinations are contained within the sheet pattern, joining them in different combinations does not produce noticible pattern variations.

> **From the single block to the sheet patterns, that means that there are numerous possible design alternatives from just one individual block .**

So much value from only one little Paradise Flower block .... and so easy to draft a billion others ...... and combine them ..... all your own original blocks ...... and easy to sew together too .... Heaven for the patchworker .....
that's why they are called 'Paradise Flowers'!!

Who needs to copy other people's patterns ?

Practice in Using Symmetry

You are invited to photocopy this page so that you can practice arranging blocks in the previous formations. This will help to clarify the flower positions and patterns that you like best.

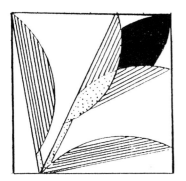 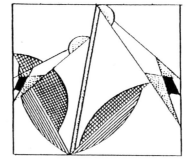 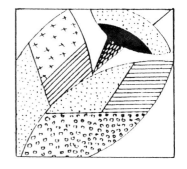

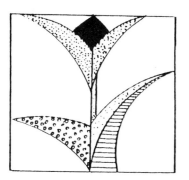  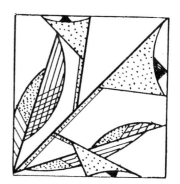

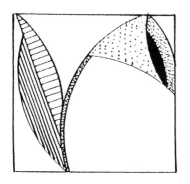 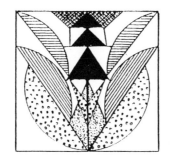 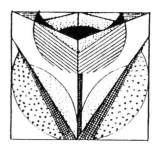

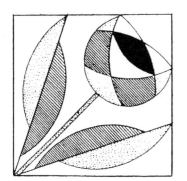 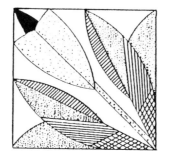 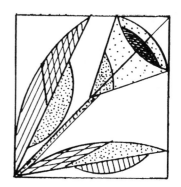

Square Blocks and Other Shapes

Another approach to creating diversity is to draft flowers inside different shapes.
The edges of the shape are always marked in numbered units as before .....
to facilitate drafting and combining.

Any shape can be used if it is to stand alone .... e.g. on a cushion front.

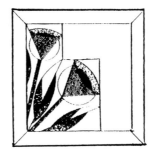

If the shapes are required to join together edge to edge .... to cover a surface ....
i.e. to tessellate ...
(so called after Roman mosaics made from small tiles or 'tesserae ')
forming either a regular, or irregular repeating pattern, then the options are
more limited.

> Irregular shapes will tessellate in a random fashion ... rather like the
> units of a crazy quilt design. Individual shapes with matching edges
> need to be worked out as you go.
> There are too many possible combinations to make guidelines practical.

Regular shapes which repeat in a predictable way are the most useful for our
purposes.

Squares ...... are always the most basic and useful shape.
Squares will tessellate in **six** different ways............

1. **Edge to edge**.......

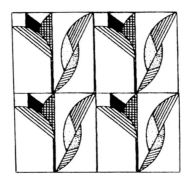

2. Brick wall .... each square starts half way along the one below. This alternative will have rows ending in half squares.

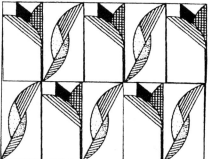
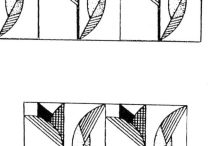

3. Staggered .... similar to brick wall, but the amount of overlap can be varied by offsetting squares by differing amounts.

The marked side intervals serve as a placement guide.
This configuration will result in a stepped effect at the ends of rows.

4. Combining different sized squares. ......
It is easy to draft half, or quarter sized squares, providing that the dimensions of the largest block are easily divisible by two or four.
Unrelated sizes may leave gaps which can be tessellated with filler shapes.
Matching them to the background will camouflage them.

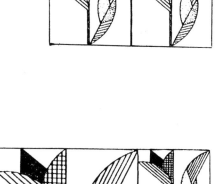

5. Modified squares .... If opposing sides of a square are altered in the same way, the newly created shape will also tessellate.
The easiest way to do this is to align a plate with two corners of the square and draw the top curve inside the square and the base curve outside.

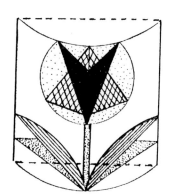

6.   Divided squares ....

Squares can be subdivided in several ways, allowing flower designs to be included in some areas and not others.

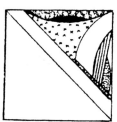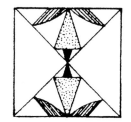

a. The square with modified sides could be further subdivided ....
e.g. by drawing another curve inside the new shape.
This could be used as an area of plain fabric between flower patterns.

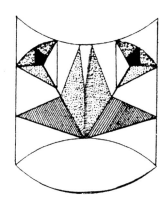

b.   The central area can be subdivided in other ways too .....

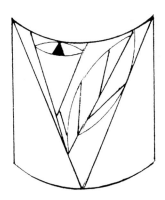

Combining these divided blocks can create interesting secondary original patterns.

These will still be easy to draft and sew together.

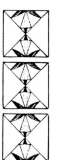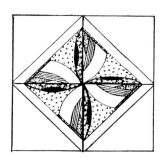

Rectangles

Rectangles are just as useful as squares .... they can be rotated, flipped, staggered, modified and divided in the same way.

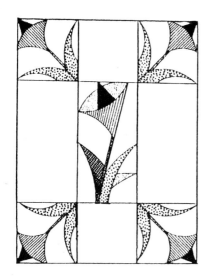

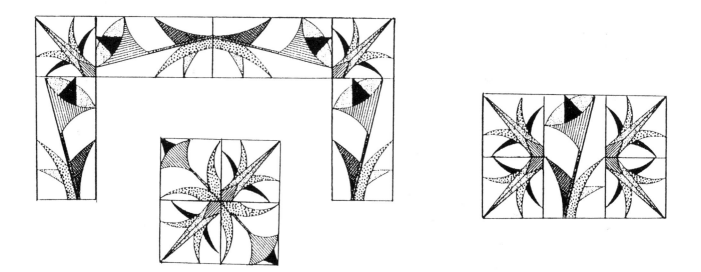

Flipped rectangles can make lovely border designs .... especially if they contain curves which contrast with the straight edges of the quilt.

'Paradise Flower' by *Angela Madden*
33ins. x 27ins.

Detail.

45

Table runner. 55ins. x 20ins.

Matching table mat.

Circle Sliced designs.

Hexagon. **19in. diameter.**
Sue Martin.

Pentagon … **30in. diameter**
by Michele Maloney.
Chiswell Green. Herts

Wallhanging by Alison King.
St. Albans. Herts.
40ins. x 12ins.

Fast Stained Glass.

Experimenting with four blocks. (Using Quick Bias)

Silk cushion by Mary Rich.
Harpenden. Herts.
16 1/2ins. x 16 1/2ins. (Using Quick Bias)

Detail.

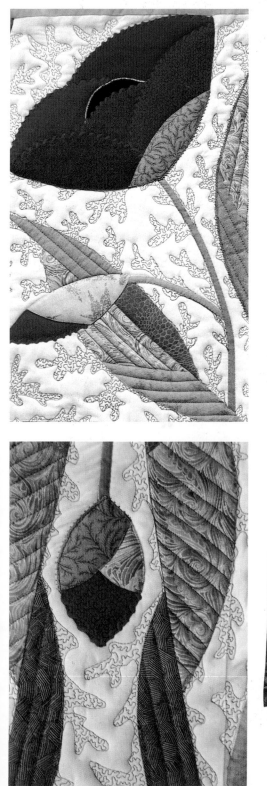

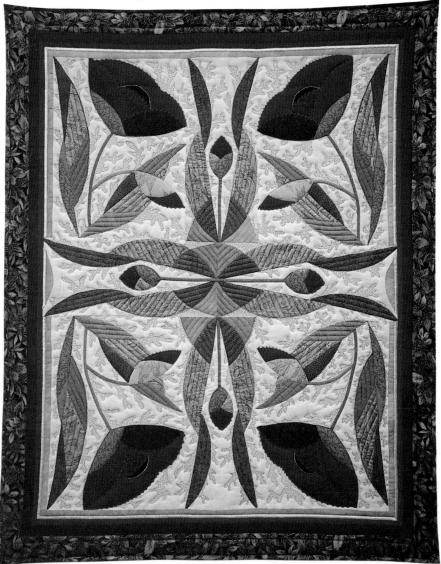

'In Praise of Poppies' by Angela Madden.
36ins. x 44ins.

**Note the use of automatic
machine embroidery stitches.**

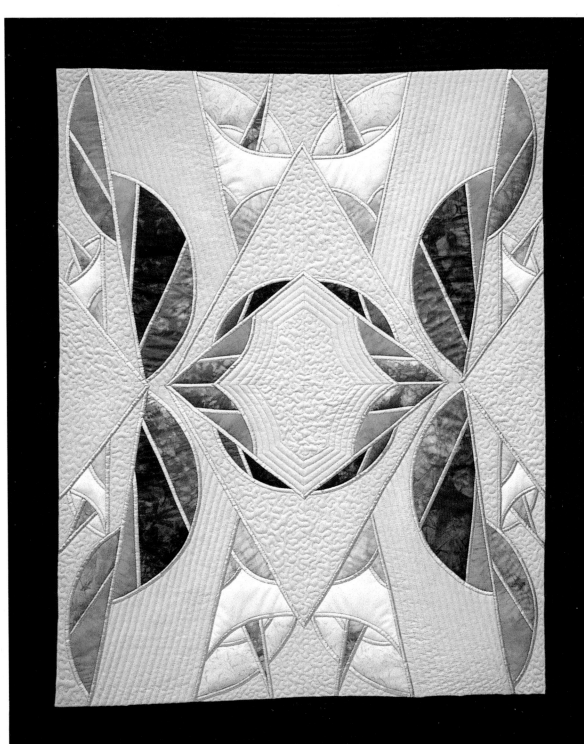

'Nouveau Lilies'
by

Angela Madden.

45ins. x 38ins.
Uses 'Quick Bias'

Quilted Firescreen by Judy Wilson. Wheathampstead. Herts.

Height 35ins. x length 47ins.
Stained glass using knitting ribbon leading.

Stencilled Designs.

Wallhanging by Kathleen McMahon.
Watford. Herts.
22ins. x 13 1/2ins.

Spacer Designs

The gaps that can occur when rectangles and squares are assembled together can be filled with plain fabric or ... it is very easy and efficient to create one or more 'spacer designs' while you are designing the original square or rectangular blocks.

These spacer designs can be fitted between linked blocks, like sashing, to create further design variations ... or ... used as matching borders if the same flower used in the block is repeated.

They can be pieced in the same way as the main design ....
or used as quilting patterns on plain fabric to provide contrast.

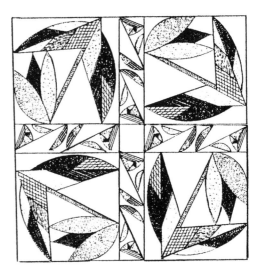

Draft the block shape on a piece of scrap paper large enough to accommodate an extension shape.

Add the extra shape (s) onto the side (s) of the main block...............
marking the numbered intervals in the usual way.

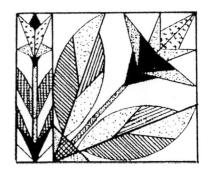

Leaves and flowers are drafted as before.

53

Using Hexagons

Regular hexagons have been sewn together in fabric as long as quilts have been made. This figure, with six equal length sides, will tessellate exactly into sheets .... therefore, a flower design could be drafted inside creating a single medallion .... or hexagons could be joined together forming composite patterns.

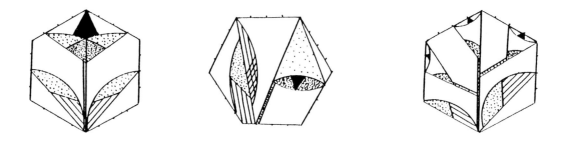

Because hexagons have six different sides, (as opposed to four with squares and rectangles) .... more pattern options are possible when different combinations are linked. Hexagons are harder to join into rows by machine.........
as stitching would involve changing direction mid seam.
However, if the hexagon has an additional background triangle added at each corner .... transforming it into a rectangle .... the problem is solved.

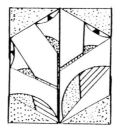

Hexagons can be created by joining six equilateral triangles in a circle. Joining these triangles in multiples of three to form half hexagons ....
and in turn sewing these together to form rows, also removes the construction problems involved in joining hexagons.

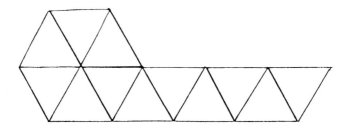

The Versatile Equilateral Triangle

Triangles can be used alone or combined to create other larger shapes.......
(See page 60 for easy drafting instructions for equilateral triangles using the 'Circle Slice Ruler')

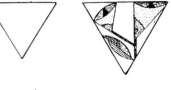

a. One equilateral triangle inverted on another creates a diamond.

This can be used on its own as a medallion, or combined with other triangles or diamonds.

b. 6 triangles will combine to form a hexagon shaped block.

c. 8 triangles will combine forming a composite diamond.

d. 9 triangles will combine forming a composite triangle.

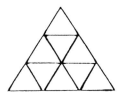

e. 12 triangles combine into a star.

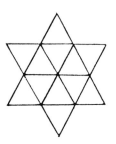

f. They also make beautiful borders.

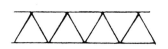

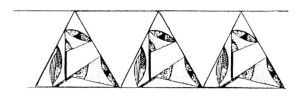

Equilateral triangles are wonderfully useful shapes because it is possible to match any side of one triangle with any side of its neighbour.
Patterns drafted within such triangles are either......
  a. Symmetrical patterns ....   **or** ....   **b. Asymmetrical patterns.**

They behave differently in combination.
Symmetrical patterns have fewer options since
by definition two sides are the same ..... but reversed.
There is therefore little point in creating flipped
mirror images of these designs.

Six equilateral triangles naturally combine into a hexagon.
There are four possible pattern combinations within a single hexagon ....
(six ... if you consider that two designs will also rotate in the opposite direction)
They all use rotation ...   although one looks like it has been flipped.

They create two sheet patterns in which the paired block appears at the centre.

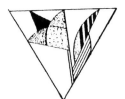

Asymmetrical patterns have more options .....
There are six possible combinations using any such design ......

and three more if you include alternate flipped versions.

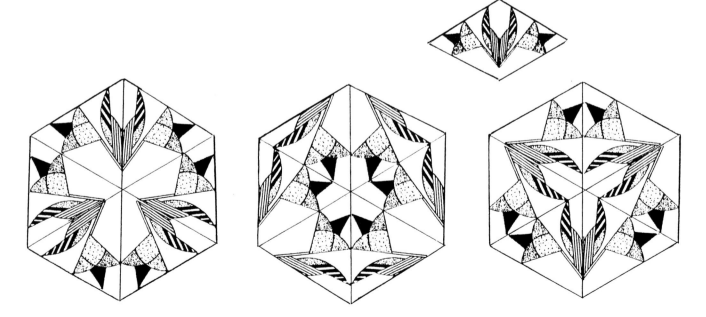

There are four possible sheet
designs created by joining
identical hexagons.

Three contain two related designs

and this one contains all three
designs containing alternately
flipped sections... X, Y and Z

Patterns created by mixing
different hexagon blocks tend
to be less harmonious as the
pattern repeats become irregular.

Drafting Equilateral Triangles .... the easy way
using the 'Circle Slice Ruler'

The 'Circle Slice Ruler' is a drafting aid which can be used in preference to a protractor when drawing precise angles for patchwork designs..

Of course it is possible to produce such angles using a protractor ... but from my own experience and also from teaching workshops ... I have found that the average patchworker is not guaranteed to be accurate in his/her usage of this tool ...... eyesight is often rightly blamed! The 'Circle Slice' eliminates this problem.

The Parts of the 'Circle Slice Ruler'.

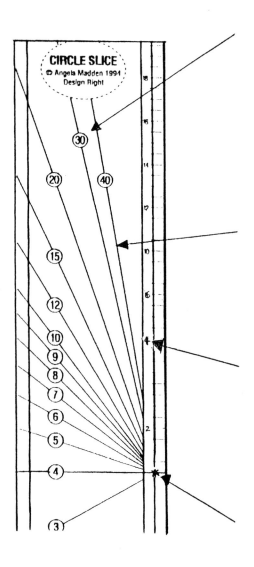

1. **The circled numbers.**
   These are the number of divisions of a circle, or slices which you can choose to include in a design.

2. **The slanting lines.**
   These set up the correct angles in conjunction with the right hand edge of the ruler, creating the number of slices you have chosen.

3. **The right hand edge measurements.**
   These are your choices for the diameter of the completed design.

4. **The star.**
   A device which enables you to check for accuracy when drafting the angles.

60

The 'Circle Slice Ruler'

This ruler is very easy to use. It is no longer necessary to think in terms of the number of degrees contained in an angle since it replaces a protractor.

e.g. Previously if you wished to slice up a circle into six equal segments you would divide 360 degrees by six ... making each central angle 60 degrees. The protractor would then be used to draft this precise angle to create a triangle. Joining six of these triangles in a circle would form a hexagon.

While using the 'Circle Slice' it is not necessary to consider degrees at all.
Instead .... think 'slices', as in dividing up a pie.

Make your choice of how many slices you wish to include in your design ....
in this case six .... from the circled numbers printed centrally on the ruler.
The circled number 6 will give you the correctly drafted angle for six slices ...
the circled 15 for fifteen slices and so on.

The 'Circle Slice' is designed to draft from the straight edge of a sheet of paper.
Use a mechanical, fine lead pencil to ensure that all lines are of a uniform width.
Using a pencil with a thick lead decreases accuracy.

Drawing the angle.

The 'Circle Slice' has been designed for right handed use.
All diagrams are therefore shown in this way.

However by ....
> turning it over,
> using it 'back to front',
> rotating it anti- clockwise,
> and using the right hand edge of the paper,

left handed use is easily facilitated.

1. Always begin to draft with the ruler right side up. Rotate the end furthest from you clockwise, until the circled number that you have chosen and the slanting line passing through it, lie exactly along the left hand edge of the paper,

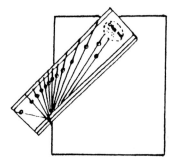

2. It is essential that the star on the ruler is placed centrally on the paper's edge. This will ensure that the ruler is properly aligned for accuracy.

To draft the six slice angle....

3. Draw a line along the right side of the ruler, from the edge of the paper to the diameter measurement you choose .. ... A to B.
The correct angle for your slice is always the one which is currently underneath the ruler.

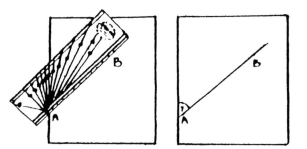

4. Measuring the Diameter .....

1. This should be thought of as a completely separate action ....
requiring re-alignment of the ruler. Use the measurements along the right hand side of the ruler ...... placing the ruler's edge on top of the line that you have drawn.

2. Start measuring from where the measurements begin on the ruler ....
at the end of the line containing the star ...... placed on the start of the pencil line at the paper's edge .... A .... which marks the centre of the circle.

3. Mark the diameter measurement of your choice .... C.

Please Note .... Diameter measurements are used at face value, with no further calculations involved. The numbers on the ruler rise in two inch stages, whilst the space between them is only one inch. This is because the ruler actually measures the radius of the circle. This figure is doubled to allow for the radius of the other half circle.

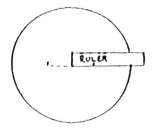

- Diameters of up to 20 ins can be drafted using the ruler ....
if a greater diameter is required add another ruler alongside the 'Circle Slice' to extend the line to the required length.
- Remember that for every inch on the other ruler, two inches will be added to the diameter of the circle .... or hexagon these assembled triangles will form.
-This diameter measurement will only be truly accurate measured across from point to point on the hexagon.

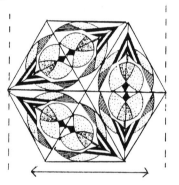

4. To mark the diameter on the other side of the triangle, butt the ruler against the edge of the paper. Match the right hand end of the star line to point A, as before. Mark the same diameter on the paper's edge ... D.

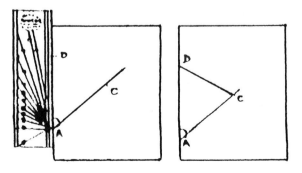

5. Join D C with a straight line to complete the top of the slice which will be an equilateral triangle.

The 'Circle Slice Ruler' can also be used to draft other triangular 'slices' which will combine into other many sided figures. Once again the central angle is correctly obtained by lining up the circled number corresponding to the number of slices that you wish to use, on the edge of the paper.

Slices making up other figures can be varied by alternative positioning of the flower within the slice.

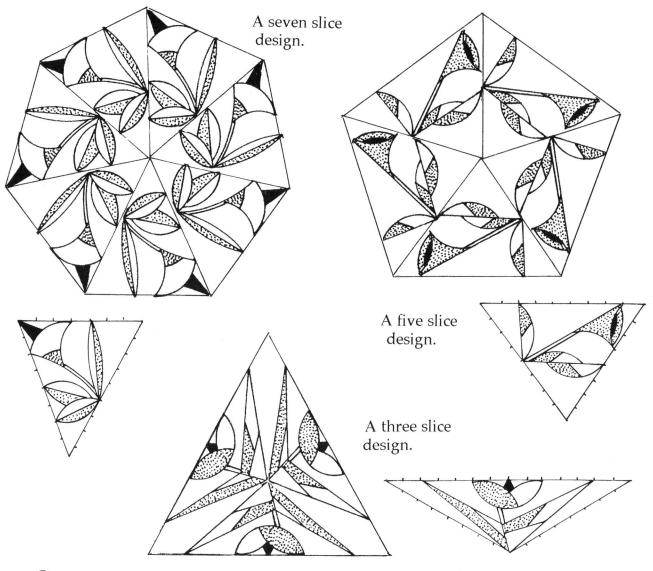

A seven slice design.

A five slice design.

A three slice design.

A final comment on the exercise of playing with design......

Yes ..... it may take longer than buying a ready made pattern and templates for a pre - designed quilt. However, not only will the result of playing be a pattern truly original to you ... the chosen design will be the one that really appeals to you .... and you may find the design exercise fascinating and enjoyable in itself, as it is full of surprises. It can be very therapeutic and relaxing.

The new understanding it brings will increase confidence in your own design skills and cause you to look at other people's quilts in books and shows with new interest.

Templates

The assembly of pieced and stained glass projects containing more than one identical block can be speeded up by multiple cutting the freezer paper templates at the same time.
Here's how ....

When the scrap paper design is completed, I usually enhance the pencil lines with felt pen to make them clear.

Photocopy enlarging the scrap design is the fastest, most efficient way to bigger projects. If the required size is greater than the machine can process at one go .... halve, or quarter, the scrap design and individually enlarge each section ..... before sticking it together again with clear tape.

For patchwork piecing you will need........

At least **three copies** of the design at the correct size ..... on ordinary paper.
1 accurate copy   to cut through when creating the freezer paper templates.
1 copy to which fabric pieces can be pinned to when they have been cut out.
1 copy to view as your master copy for reference whilst you sew.
The last two copies can be traced or needle punched copies. (see page 64.)

Number each shape identically on each copy
Other techniques require different numbers of copies.
These are dealt with in the appropriate section.

---

1.   Decide on the number of blocks required.
Cut one piece of freezer paper for each block ....
approx. 1/2 inch larger all round .... than the finished block size.

(This extra allowance is insurance ... you can always cut an extra bit off ... but you cannot add it on if you are short ... and it happens to us all at times !!!)

Tip.

While freezer paper templates remain ironed to the fabric they act as an effective stabiliser and aid handling. Bias edges cannot stretch or distort. Shapes can therefore be cut from fabric without regard to the grain lines. This facilitates the economic use of fabric. However, when making items intended for show, or for 'that special heirloom' it is easy to follow the grain if you wish.
Drawing coloured lines at intervals on the freezer paper before it is cut up will prevent small pieces getting turned around ... and can also be grain line indicators.

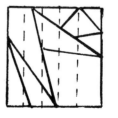

---

2. Decide if you wish to include flipped blocks.

3. Stack all the freezer papers, checking the direction in which the shiny side is facing ....

For patchwork piecing using flipped images ...

Freezer paper should be stacked ....
shiny side up for designs duplicating the copy ...
dull side up for designs flipping the copy.
The same number of each should be cut.

---

4. Place the accurate design copy on the top of the stack .... and pin through all layers. Position one pin in each shape large enough to take one.

If you are using a lot of blocks and require many layers of freezer paper,
you might need to do this in batches of four at a time ...
so that all the layers will not be too difficult to pin or cut through at once.

Each batch after the first will require one extra accurate design copy to cut up.

5. Lay the pinned stack of papers on a cutting board and rotary cut around the design shapes, through all layers at once.
Paper shapes must be cut apart very accurately as they will be used as templates.
No seam allowance has been included during drafting.
Use a rotary ruler to guide the cutter on straight lines ....
and cut curves freehand. Cutting curves is easy if it is
done in short cuts. Use cutter blades which are past
their razor sharp best for this job, as cutting paper will
dull the blade.The advantage of using a rotary cutter is
that all pressure is applied from the top and the layers
are therefore less inclined to slide one over another,
which would result in cutting slightly different versions
of the same shape.
Extend your index finger to guide the cutter ...
and raise your wrist to press downwards efficiently.

It is also possible to cut the freezer paper layers with scissors ..... provided that the blades are very sharp and do not cause the layers to shift during cutting.

6. As multiples of each shape are separated from the rest, pin the papers in position on the second design copy for easy identification.

7. Numbering them individually on the dull side is also a good idea, in case one gets separated from its fellows.

8. Label those which are flipped. (I add 'F' for flipped to the piece number.)

7. Iron the shaped paper templates to the wrong side of the chosen fabric ....

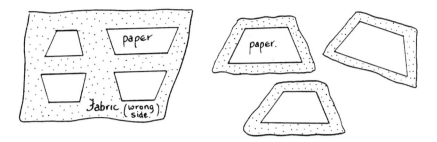

8. Cut out each shape allowing approx 1/4 in. all around.

9. Sort them into designs and flipped designs .....
stack and label them and re - pin to the design copy ....
in the correct position ready for stitching.

It will then be possible to speed up assembly by sewing the same shape to its neighbour throughout all blocks, by working through two adjoining stacks ....
rather than completing one whole block before starting on the next.

Speciality designs .... e.g. border prints, can be used to great effect in both single and flipped shapes. Papers can be strategically placed to enhance mirror images. Individual petals and leaves can gain character and importance from the particular patterns they contain. Pattern should always take precedence over grain when using directional prints.

Fabric Requirements .....

It is impossible to give precise yardage for individual flower designs, since by their very nature they are all different ..... original to the person creating them.

Variables can be ...

     the number of shapes used.
     the size of the design.
     the number of petals, leaves and background space.
     the number of fabrics used.
     the number of block repeats

Despite this, it is easy to estimate approximate needs for a block, since the shapes themselves provide a clear visual guide to the requirements when laid on the fabric.

Multiply by the number of block repeats.
Fabric variety will enhance designs ... so if you run out of one fabric, use another!
Match the colour tone and it will look fine.

Trouble Free Piecing

There is little point in being able to create beautiful flower designs if sewing them together is troublesome or ends in an unsatisfactory result. That is when a current project becomes a U.F.O. (unfinished object) and often remains so !

Paradise Flowers will fit together like a jig - saw puzzle, if they have been cut apart accurately. Ensure that the different shapes are laid out in the right order before sewing. Numbered shapes can be checked against the master copy to ensure that they are correctly placed in each block.
Remember that piecing the block will reverse the duplicated paper design.

General sewing guidelines.

There is no specific sewing order that can be applied to every design .....
- generally **small pieces** are sewn together to make **big pieces** .....
- **big pieces** are sewn together to create **bigger pieces** ...... and ....
- **bigger pieces** are sewn to **bigger pieces** to complete the block.

Straight seams are sewn as usual, from the back of the work ... and curved seams are all sewn from the front. Freezer paper is left on throughout the stitching and only removed when the block has been completed.

If a long seam runs across two or three short seams, it makes sense to sew the short ones together first .... them complete the longer seam

All straight seams are sewn as follows ....

1. Match two adjoining fabric shapes with freezer paper still attached, right sides facing, ready to pin the seam which is to be joined.

2. Insert a pin through the fabric on the first shape, from the wrong side, at one end of the freezer paper. (Long fine pins are best.)

3. Align the second shape behind the first, so that the point of the pin exits at the matching point to its entry.

4. Push half the length of the pin into the seam, leaving it sticking straight out.

5. Repeat with another pin at the other end.

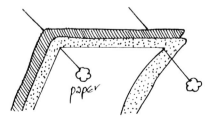

6.   If the seam is a long one, it may be necessary to insert one or more pins between the previous two. These should be inserted at the edge of the paper, bringing both fabric sections into precise alignment. Take care not to pin through the paper itself on either side.

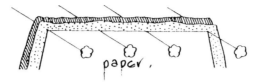

7.   Re - insert the full length of the two outer pins .... facing points inwards towards each other. Do this as if they were needles performing little running stitches along the edge of the paper. If additional pins have been used, face them all towards the left, running them along in the same manner.

8.   I can achieve greater accuracy by completing straight seams in two stages, starting to sew from part way along and continuing to each end in turn, as follows ....

9.   Begin to stitch the seam in the space between opposite facing pins, travelling beside the paper to the end of the fabric. Use a stitch length which is a compromise between being small enough to be secure .... and being large enough to be undone without much difficulty, should the need arise.

10.   As you stitch, hold the head of the pin immediately in front of the machine needle. It will extend towards you and is easy to grasp ....
.... do not pull the pin out ....
hold it in a constant position, allowing it to be withdrawn gradually as the fabric is moved away from you by the action of the machine feed dogs.

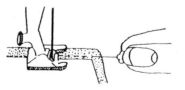

The pin will continue to anchor the fabric in the correct position for as long as possible, just in front of the needle .... without the risk of hitting it. Remove all pins in turn in this way.

11. When the first stitching is complete, flip the shapes over to stitch the open end of the seam. Always over sew 1/4 in. of the previous stitching to lock the threads.

12. Trim any loose ends and the seam allowances to a neat 1/4 in. Also snip a diagonal cut across both ends of the seam allowance. This will reduce the bulk at intersections.

Stitching curves.

1. Any curve is easy to piece if it can be sewn from the right side, so that you can see exactly what is happening .... and it is possible to sew all the curves you have designed in this way !

This is always quicker and easier than sewing curved seams from the back, and enables everyone .... even a novice sewer, to get a great result first go.

2. A curved seam always consists of a convex curve and a concave curve. Convex curves always have the seam allowance folded under to the wrong side before stitching .... and are always sewn **on top of** the corresponding concave curve.
This allows the concave seam allowance to lie flat.

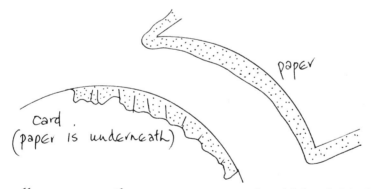

The seam allowance on the convex curves should be folded over the edge of the paper and pressed in place. A piece of cereal packet weight cardboard, cut to the same curve and temporarily laid on top of the edge of the paper, will ensure a perfectly folded fabric curve.

3. All cotton fabrics will remain flat when folded and pressed using a moderately hot iron, if the 'fold' is lightly water dampened with the touch of a 'cotton bud' or wet finger. Difficult fabrics or those containing man made fibre will need to be anchored down with a re-positionable adhesive such as 'Spray Mount"

4. The two curves can be matched for sewing by holding them up to the light in your sewing machine, so that you can see the edge of the freezer paper through the fabric. The folded curve can then be correctly aligned on the right side ......
or .....   by sticking pins through the concave allowance from the back, just at the paper's edge .... then lining up the folded edge with the entry point on the front.

The exit point of the pins shows the position of the freezer paper on the other side.

Wrong side view.   Right side view.

5. If a piece of scrap paper is placed behind the curves as they are lined up, it becomes easy to pin them in place .... through the scrap paper .....
from the right side of the convex shape into the concave seam allowance.

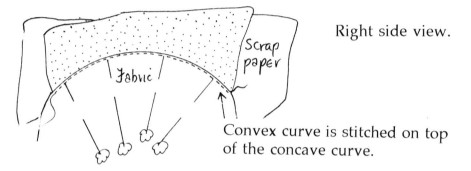

Right side view.

Convex curve is stitched on top of the concave curve.

Take care that the pin points do not overlap the folded edge of the fabric, so that they will not have to be moved during the stitching.

6.   The seam can now be straight stitched on the machine, following the curve, as near to the edge as possible .... using .....
    a.   a shorter than usual stitch ..... stitch length 1· 5
    b. transparent thread ... ('clear' on light fabrics and 'smoke' on dark)....
    c. a fine (no. 60) needle ...... so that the stitches 'disappear' into the fabric.
These needles are not utility sewing needles as they break very easily. They are designed to be used for specialist purposes, where small holes are required.
Sewn in this way the curve will look very similar to a pieced seam. It will take close scrutiny to discern the difference.

7. Variety can be added by ignoring the preceeding instructions and sewing over the curve using one of the automatic embroidery stitches and a fancy embroidery thread. This can serve to enhance and embellish the curves.
Using an automatic wavy satin stitch can give the appearance of a frilled edge to a petal .... or a picot edge to a leaf ..... and a contrasting or variegated coloured thread can highlight an edge .... or link it to a machine embroidered flower centre. If this decorative stitching is completed through all layers .... top, wadding and backing at the same time .... it will quilt the item at the same time.

71

Pressing the Seams

1. After every seam has been sewn and trimmed to 1/4 in. it is important to press it before continuing. For this purpose an iron and board are usefully positioned beside the machine. Straight seams can be pressed open or to one side, usually the darker fabric side. Wherever possible seams which cross should be pressed in opposite directions.

2. The freezer paper can then be lifted from underneath both seam allowances, enabling them to be tucked neatly underneath the paper template.

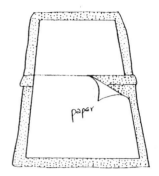

3. Replace the freezer paper on top of the seam allowances .... carefully iron it down so that the edges of the paper templates touch.

Lifting and repositioning the paper is essential for accuracy and helps in the following ways...........

1. By holding the seam allowances firmly in the chosen direction. and keeping the design perfectly flat during the construction process.

2. By firming up the pieces and making them easier to handle. The seams between small sections of the design are stiffened so that they behave like one large solid piece.

3. By highlighting slight discrepancies in alignment which may have occurred during stitching. It is easy to reposition one or both papers to restore accuracy.

    ## Yes !!...... if it is not right..... move the paper !!!

    ## When the item is finished no one will ever know.

    ## This is _not_ cheating .... _it is efficiency !_

4. By keeping the design perfectly flat during the construction process.

5. By keeping all the template edges clearly visible .... when all seams are sewn the paper design will have re - formed on the back like a jig - saw puzzle. With all edges aligned, finished designs will be guaranteed to be the correct size.

---

4. Complete the block ... trim the outer edges to 1/4in. .... and then use it to complete your chosen item

Three Dimensional Flowers

Flower centres, or other areas of these designs, are ideal places for adding 3D ....
embroidered .... or beaded embellishments ......

- Small tassels can become stamens......

- ribbon embroidery can be flower centres

- crystals can be dew drops............

- beads can become seeds or insects....

- twisted cords can be couched in place instead of pieced stalks

.... in fact anything that takes your fancy can be included.

- 'Prairie points' made from fabric or ribbon,can also be inserted in seams
in the same way. The use of satin ribbon adds a nice sheen which contrasts with
the matt fabric.

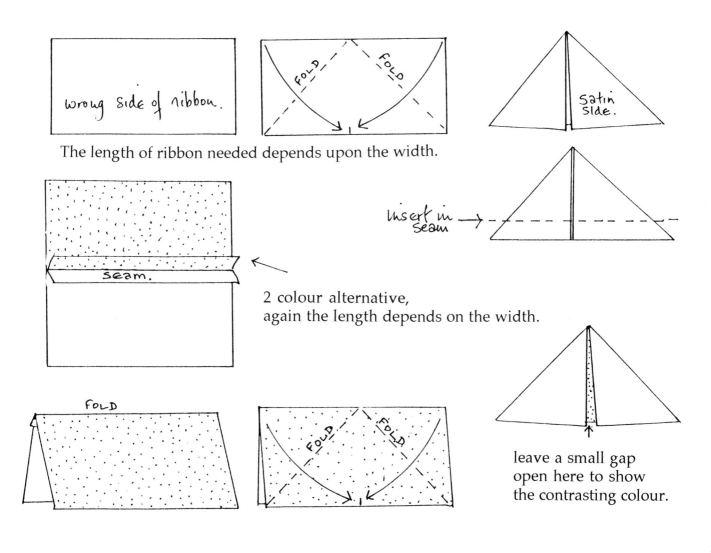

The length of ribbon needed depends upon the width.

2 colour alternative,
again the length depends on the width.

leave a small gap
open here to show
the contrasting colour.

Stained Glass Flowers

Paradise Flowers are ideally combined with the patchwork 'stained glass' technique. Once again freezer paper is the key to transforming your own unique designs into wonderful items in this classic style.
The resulting patterns can be similar to many authentic window panels, or you can 'do your own thing' entirely.

The designs of Charles Rennie Mackintosh .... (though not all in stained glass) may be of interest as an inspiration source in this context, as similar panels are really easy to create. The resulting designs need not be copies, but can be completely original to you, but 'in the style of the above ....

(I wonder if C. R. M. used saucers to draft his roses ? .... you never know!)

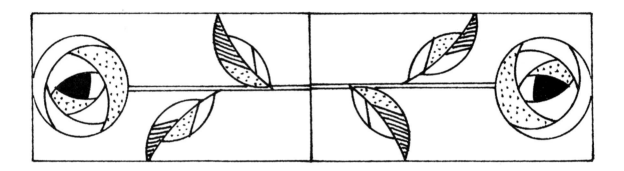

Whilst it is perfectly possible to cut and sew your own bias tubing to act as the 'mock leading' between the different coloured sections, covering the joins, the recent innovation of store bought 'Quick Bias '^{TM} tape, (ready cut and folded, with fusible already applied to the back, for easy placement before sewing) makes this technique easier than ever before. This tape is produced in many different solid colours. The use of black, or navy blue will create an authentic stained glass effect, while gold is particularly valuable for creating 'Cloisonné' style designs.

'Cloisonné' is the name given to the enamelling technique in which a shiny gold wire is placed between shaped sections containing bright coloured enamels. The wire is the equivalent of the leading placed between the different shapes in stained glass windows.

Decorative machine stitching, or satin stitch can also be substituted for bias to cover the fabric join. Wavy versions look very effective providing a novel fluted edge to petals. Do, however, check that all raw edges are well secured.

'Cloisonné'is ideally suited to flower patterns. Both the real thing and the fabric version look very rich and reflect light beautifully.........
(Oh, I do love a 'bit of glitz'!)

If stained glass designs are assembled ……. but left unquilted …….. they can look stunning hung against a window, as with this technique the reverse side is not unsightly. Such a panel would make a memorable roller blind, or transform an ugly view. Unpatterned fabric looks the most authentic.

Of course they can also be beautifully quilted into cushions, quilts, wallhangings and wearable art in the normal way .

1. For this technique you will need three copies of the design. Follow page 65 points 1 to 6 inclusive, but this time placing the freezer paper…….

> **For stained glass**
> dull side up for designs duplicating the copy...
> shiny side up for designs flipping the copy.

2. Iron the paper templates to **<u>the right side of the fabric .</u>** Individual shapes can be placed closely together as no seam allowance is required between them... except for edges of shapes on the outside of the block, where the extra 1/2 in. insurance has been added.

3. Cut out the fabric shapes exactly around the paper templates.

4. As Fusi - knit^{TM} is required for this technique, make sure that you are familiar with the information on p 6.

The Fusi - knit^{TM} should be cut at least 1 in. larger than the required size of the finished item.

If this necessitates the joining of pieces together, avoid having overlaps or sewn seam allowances by temporarily taping the join. Use clear tape, sticking it to the non - fusible side. Overlaps would cause unsightly bumps in the finished item.

Make sure that the join is taped throughout its length, with no gaps to curl up and become a nuisance.

The tape can be removed later on when the Fusi - knit^{TM} is fused onto the fabric.

> **<u>Tip</u>**
>
> Do check that the clear tape you intend to use will not melt when exposed to the heat of an iron. This is easily done by clear taping a piece of scrap paper and ironing over it …… if nothing happens to the tape, it is fine to use.
> Iron temperature is often a crucial factor.

5. Place the master pattern face upwards on an ironing board ....
or, better still, a piece of soft board kept specially for such jobs as this.
A separate board is really useful as it can be cut to a more convenient size, wider than the average ironing board. It will enable the entire project to become portable for storage or convenience during the laying out process, without disturbing work in progress.

Such a board can be fabric covered and stood on end to view work from a distance, something you must do frequently in order to judge the overall effect.

Admiring work in progress helps to spur you on!

6. Lay the Fusi - knit ^{TM} over the master pattern with the fusible side upwards.
Pin it over .... **but not to** the pattern .... onto the board underneath.
Make sure that there are no wrinkles or distortions.
It should be flat, but not stretched.

7. Because the Fusi - knit ^{TM} is transparent, the master pattern will be clearly visible underneath. This enables each fabric shape to be accurately placed, edge to edge, in the correct position over the master copy.......
just like assembling the pieces of a jig - saw puzzle.

8. Gently dry iron each fabric shape in place.

9. As each individual shape is positioned securely ...... remove the freezer paper.

10. When all the shapes are firmly in place, the bias can be ironed centrally over each join to cover the raw edges. Be careful with the order in which the bias is applied to ensure that cut ends of short bias strips are hidden under long pieces. Always place the upright of a T - junction first and the cross bar second.
Cut ends should only be visible at the edges of the block.

11. Both sides of the bias must be stitched down throughout the design. The fusible backing (either on Quick Bias ^{TM} or the Bondaweb ^{TM} used with home made bias) will not withstand washing and wear.

There are three alternative stitches which could be used......

a. Blind hem stitch ......   with both stitch length and width reduced to between 1 5 and 1. The minute zig zag nips the bias edge, while the straight stitch falls on the background.

b. Straight stitch along the edges ... a short stitch to look good.

c. Zig zag ... 'zigging' onto the bias, and 'zagging' off it, again sized to look good.

A size 60 needle and good quality transparent thread will render the above almost invisible.

Fast Stained Glass

This is a really fast way to put together a stained glass flower design. It works on the principle of 'robbing Peter to pay Paul'. Multiple cutting several layers of fabric at once ensures that a shape cut from one colour will fit into the matching hole in another.

1. Decide on the number of different colours you wish to use. This may coincide with the the number of blocks required, or alternatively you might choose to work with a limited number of colours and repeat them.
The number of shapes in the design should be divisible by the number of fabric colours.
In designs containing flipped blocks, plain fabrics which do not have a right and wrong side are the most versatile choice. Individual cut shapes can then be used either side up to increase the colour variety possible between blocks. (Removing the freezer paper if is placed on the inconvenient side of the fabric)

It is vital to have contrasts between the chosen colours so that the pattern shapes will be clearly visible.

2. Cut a piece of each fabric to the planned finished block size, plus 1/2 in. extra all round. The number of fabric pieces will equal the number of finished blocks you can make using this method.

3. Cut one piece of freezer paper for each piece of fabric to the same size.

4. Iron the freezer paper onto the right side of the fabric.

5. As before you will need three copies of the design ... stack all the fabric the same way up with one copy of the design on top.

6. Pin the stack together placing a pin in each design shape.

7. Rotary cut on the design lines, through all the stacked fabric. It is vital for this technique that there is no slipping ... or the different shapes will not fit.

8. Pin each stacked shape in the correct place on the second design copy.

9. Lay out all blocks before you start fusing any of them (so that you don't end up with two pink pieces together in the last block.
Follow page 76 instructions 5 to 11 to complete each block.

Bias Appliqué.

Since very detailed instructions for this technique appear in two of my previous books ('Sew Easy Celtic' and 'Magic Celtic') a shortened version is now provided.

1. Establish bias requirements by laying a length of wool over the joins which are to be covered.

2. To estimate the bias yield from a given square consult the following table. It applies to bias cut at 1in. wide. (Strip width needs to be twice the finished width plus 1/4in for seam allowance.)

Square.	Bias.	Square.	Bias.	Square.	Bias.	Square.	Bias.
8in. =	50ins.	9in. =	72in.	10 1/2 in. =	98in.	12in. =	128in.
13 1/2 in. =	162in.	15in =	200in.	16 1/2 in. =	242in.	17 1/2 in. =	288in.
19in. =	338in.	20 1/2 in =	392in.				

3. Depending upon the size of the finished block ... the individual lengths of bias needed will vary. If you wish to avoid visible joins, it will be necessary to start with a piece of fabric large enough to yield sufficient continuous lengths to complete the longer runs in the design.

4. Having decided upon the size of the fabric square required, use the 45 degree angle marked on rotary rulers to rotary cut the square diagonally on the bias.

5. Place the resulting cut triangles one on top of the other.

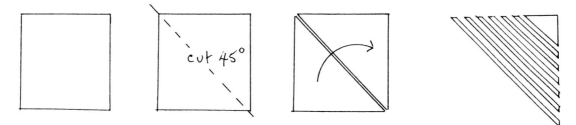

6. Rotary cut bias strips of the chosen width, parallel to the diagonal edge of the fabric. There will be wastage if the shorter strips cannot be used in your design.

7. Continuous bias binding can be easily sewn, and this is less wasteful but has visible joins. Here's how .....
a. Cut a fabric square as before....... cut diagonally at 45 degrees corner to corner.

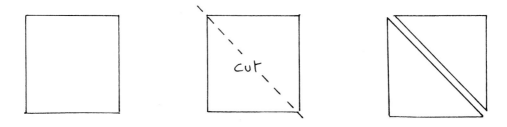

b. Sew the two triangles right sides together, having repositioned them to form a parallelogram ....
on which you now draw parallel lines along the length.
These lines should be double the width of the proposed bias plus 1/4in. (1/8in. x 2 seam allowances
for later sewing the strip into a tube.)
Press seam allowance to one side.

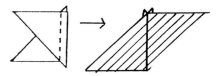

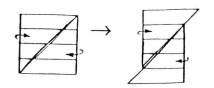

c. Curl the parallelogram as if to form a cylinder, sliding one end against the other so the lines are displaced by one line. (There will be a spare width top and bottom)
Pin and sew in this position, making sure all the seam allowances are on the outside of the cylinder.

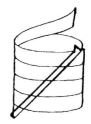

d. Cut along the drawn lines, creating a continuous length of binding. Press all seam allowances to same side.

Sewing bias into tubes.

1. Fold fabric strip(s) in half lengthwise ... right side out.

2. Place a flat sided magnet by the side of the machine foot to prevent the tube from altering its position as it is sewn.
The distance from the needle to the magnet should match both the size of the bias bar being used and the required tube.
(f you are worried about using a magnet with a computerised machine consult your dealer)

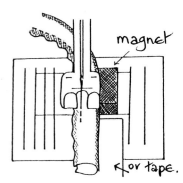

magnet

or tape.

3. Place the fabric fold next to the magnet and sew along the length of the fabric strip. Check that the chosen bias bar will fit snugly inside the stitched tube before continuing.

4. Trim the seam allowance which will be approx. 1/8 in. ...
to approximately 1/16 in. from the stitching.

5. Press the dampened tube flat, with the seam at the centre back, by slipping the bias bar inside and gently feeding the fabric off at one end to be immediately ironed. The bar will only feed down the tube in the same direction as the seam allowances have been pressed. The minute seam allowance is pressed to one side.

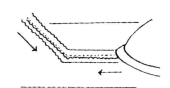

6. Dry iron strips cut 1/4in. wide of Bondaweb,^{TM} (fusible webbing on a backing paper) to the seamed side of the tube.
(To increase the adhesion of the webbing to the paper making handling easier ...
lay a length of Bondaweb,^{TM}fusible side down on a Teflon^{TM}ironing sheet and lightly iron with a warm dry iron. Place in a freezer for a minute or so to become cold before cutting into strips.)

7. Follow the Stained glass instructions starting on page 75.

Duplicating Patterns

There is another easy way to duplicate Paradise Flower patterns. This method is useful for creating extra copies where the multiple cutting of shapes is not required.

As before, the design is first drafted on scrap paper and enlarged using a photocopier if necessary.

1. Establish the number of duplicate copies required to complete the item.
Cut that number of pieces of freezer paper at least one inch larger all round than the intended design.

2. In patterns requiring **mirror images,** clarify the number of flips necessary to complete the pattern ....
turn that number of freezer paper pieces so that the dull side is uppermost ...
and the same number shiny side uppermost.
If making **exact copies** ... i.e. no flips ..... turn all the freezer papers shiny side up.

Stack them in a pile.

3. Paper clip all the freezer papers together, placing the master pattern face up on the top.

4. Remove the thread from both the bobbin and needle of your sewing machine.

5. Using a used machine needle .... (as sewing through the paper layers will dull a new needle) .... sew accurately over every line in your design through all the paper layers at once.

You will find that the holes you are making will anchor the paper layers firmly together and prevent them sliding out of position. The individual layers can later be peeled apart as required.

Check the design from the back, as it is easier to see from that side, if you have missed any pattern lines.

6. Number each design shape on the master copy .... transfer these numbers to all duplicated copies, as they are required.

7. Flipped copies can be labelled with an F next to the shape number,

8. These needle punched designs can be used in several different ways. Enhance the perforated lines with pencil if required.

9. Designs duplicated in this way can be cut into separate shapes, or stitched along the perforated lines as appropriate for the particular technique being used.

Quilted and Appliqué Flowers

1. Quilted versions of these designs can be swiftly sewn by machine. They are particularly effective using metallic or embroidery threads.
There is no need to mark the quilting lines onto the fabric ... just make a needle punched duplicate copy of the design using greaseproof or tracing paper instead of freezer paper.

a. Pin the needle punched copy of the design in place over the three layers ...
top fabric ...   wadding ...   and backing fabric .....
and machine quilt through all three along the needle punched lines.

b. When the sewing is finished, the tracing paper can very easily be torn away, as it will be perforated along all the stitching lines.

2. Another version of the above .... adding both colour and interest at the same time as quilting, is achieved by applying fabric over selected areas of the design at the same time as you quilt through all layers ....

a. Pin selected fabric pieces ...**fabric right side against the wrong side of the tracing paper.**
Each piece must entirely cover the intended design section, allowing at least 1/4 in. excess margin all around. Fabric pieces should lie flat against the paper and may sometimes overlap Cutting exact shapes is unnecessary as all excess fabric will be cut away after sewing.

Insert pins from the right side of the paper.

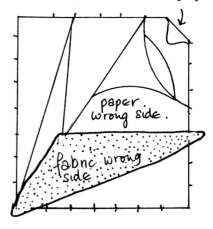

b. Insert all pins from **the right side** of the paper, so that they will be easy to reposition or remove as the sewing progresses.

c. Stack top, wadding and backing together. Place the paper design copy with fabric attached on top ... paper uppermost. Machine quilt using a straight stitch around all the design lines.

d. When the sewing is finished, remove the tracing paper. Carefully cut all excess fabric from around the outside of the appliqued shapes. Overlapped fabric can be easily removed if you cut close to the stitching **on one side only** of the excess piece.

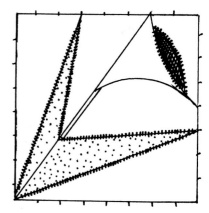

e. Satin stitch around shapes to cover the cut edges of the fabric, using matching or contrasting thread.

Trapunto

Trapunto, otherwise known as 'stuffed quilting' is another three dimensional approach to creating Paradise Flowers. An extra layer or layers of wadding are added to selected parts of the design to create greater height and a firmer feel.

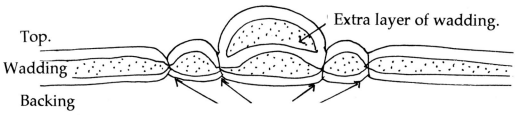

Top.

Extra layer of wadding.

Wadding

Backing

Quilting Stitching.

Trapunto designs machine stitched in a plain wholecloth .... or stencilled fabric, are a fast way to a classy result.
Here's how .....

1. Create the master and duplicate design(s) .... as described on the previous page, but use greaseproof or fine tracing paper instead of freezer paper for the duplicate copies.
Machine stitching through the paper speeds the whole process as it removes the need to mark the quilting pattern on the fabric.

2. To quilt .... pin a duplicate copy in place on the right side of the fabric.

3. Pin a piece of wadding (batting) to the back of the fabric. This must be large enough to cover the area (s) destined to be stuffed.

Tip.

The type and thickness of wadding used for this technique is optional.
A thicker wadding ... or several layers placed on top of each other
will create a firmer, harder stuffed area.
Thinner wadding will provide a softer, more gentle contrast.

Bear in mind that this wadding will only provide the stuffing in
the raised parts of the design. Here it will be additional
to the main wadding and create a double thickness.

It is recommended that you experiment with samples of wadding
of different thickness to ensure that the finished effect is to your liking.
Of course it is also possible to slit the wadding at the back after the first
stitching and insert a little extra for added 'loft'.... if you feel it is needed.
As this is done before the backing is added no one will ever know!

---

4. Machine straight stitch accurately along the design lines, around each area to be stuffed, sewing through paper .... fabric .... and wadding.
(At this stage we are not using a backing fabric)

Use transparent thread and a long stitch length for this.
This stitching line will be covered by another line of stitching later on.
The longer stitch will enable you to easily remove any stitches which are visible beside the final stitching, if it has not followed exactly the same path.

Check that each raised area is entirely surrounded by stitching with no parts left open.

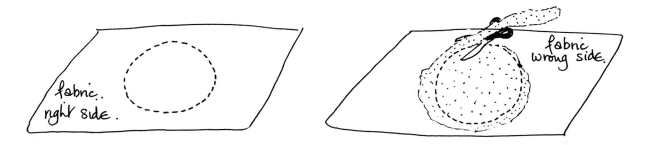

5. Remove the item from the machine ....**but do not remove the paper.**
Working from the wrong side of the work .... cut away all wadding on the outside of the stitching around each stuffed area. Be very careful not to cut through the fabric.

Try not to leave a wide margin of wadding around each shape. Ideally cut close to the stitching .... but not through it.

6. Cut away the wadding from all parts of the design except inside each area to be stuffed.

7. Lay the work, design paper uppermost, on the top of ....
     another layer of wadding (I use 2oz.) ... cut to the size of the finished item .....
     and a backing layer of fabric ....
      pinning them together, ready for quilting in the usual way.

8. Machine quilt throughout the entire piece accurately following the design lines on the paper once again,using either transparent or coloured thread. Oversew all lines including those already sewn in stage 4.

9. Remove the paper on completion of the sewing. It will easily tear along the double perforation lines.

10. The contrast between the raised features and the surrounding areas can be further increased by additional stipple quilting in selected parts.
Stippled areas will be flattened, creating textural interest.

Stencilling.

Paradise Flower designs combine beautifully with stencilling. This freezer paper technique opens up a whole new area of printing original, professional looking designs on fabric, quickly and easily .

Unlike traditional stencils, these designs do not contain 'bridges', or unpainted gaps, separating each individual painted shape, and creating the familiar stencilled appearance. 'Bridges' are vital to traditional solid stencils, enabling them to be handled as one piece. Without bridges, they would fall apart.

Using the following method the finished design looks more like a professionally screen printed fabric, with each coloured section butting up to its neighbour.

The fact that freezer paper can adhere to fabric enables individual sections to be removed temporarily from the design while the paint is applied .... then replaced to act as a mask while other areas are removed in turn and painted.

It is not necessary to stencil every single shape within a design .... picking a few selected ones can look very effective for little effort ....
e.g. colouring the flower and stalk, but not the background.

The other advantage of this technique is that designs which are too small to be comfortably pieced can be stencilled with ease .... then embellished and quilted by hand or machine into really classy items.

1. Multiple rotary cut the required number of designs, following page 66 ...... points 4 to 6 ..... as needle punched duplications will not create really sharp edges between shapes.

2. Number all shapes.

3. Use plain fabric which has been laundered to remove the sizing.

4. If the fabric is sufficiently transparent, pin the master copy underneath so that the design can be seen from the top.
A master copy in felt pen will help visibility. It will be removed before stencilling begins. If the fabric is too opaque, keep the master copy beside you, for reference.

5. Take one duplicate copy at a time .... Iron each individual paper template, to the right side of the fabric, exactly over the corresponding pattern section on the master copy, if it is visible underneath the fabric .....   or if not ....

carefully place sections edge to edge on the fabric, rebuilding the design. Never iron shapes onto the fabric at random. Rebuild the design in an orderly fashion making sure that edges are well matched to their neighbours, with no gaps or overlaps.

6. When the design is rebuilt on the fabric you can then remove individual paper shapes covering areas to be painted the same colour.

Successful stencilling is really a relatively 'dry' painting technique ....
Any paint which wets the fabric is unsuitable, as it may cause seepage under the neighbouring masking papers.
Paint is best applied very sparingly, using a brush or sponge, so that neither fabric nor paper gets wet .... or even very damp.

7. When the paint has been applied to the chosen area of fabric, the paper can be ironed back in place, on top of the paint. As the fabric is still dry, the freezer paper will re - stick without a problem.

8. Continue removing selected paper shapes, stencilling and replacing the papers until the design is complete. All papers can then be removed ....
for you to stand back and admire your handiwork!

9. Fix the paint by ironing, or in accordance with the manufacturer's instructions.

10. Spray painting is also an option for applying paint. Fade resistant colour effects can be obtained by using car paint sprays.
Colours can be mixed as the spray is applied .... or in layers on top of one another. (Always apply the lightest colour first followed by the darker shades).

If the paint is applied lightly, it will not stiffen the fabric and will dry in seconds.

Always apply the paint in short, light bursts, preventing a sticky build up on the masking paper areas. It is essential that the paper is **completely dry** before ironing .... sticky paint would attach itself to the iron. Drying may take up to 48 hours if there has been a build up of layers. Therefore, the use of this spray paint is really only suitable for colouring a limited number of areas, as the repeated removal of paper sections and successive application of paint would build up too many layers on the neighbouring masking papers.

 <u>Important .... For safety reasons,</u>
   Always use car spray paint in a very well ventilated area, or outside
   on a breeze free day. Wash fabric immediately to remove the fumes
   of the propellant gas. <u>**Do not use if you are pregnant.**</u>
   Wear a face mask and protect all surrounding surfaces.

You do run the risk of being labelled as the local graffiti artist when you purchase several different colours at once in the car spares shop. Assistants (usually young and male) are not used to having to match paint colour to fabric, flowers or pictures !......... On my last paint shopping trip the confused youth at the checkout added up the price of the seven different colours ...... took the money and finally commented .... ' I dare not ask what colour your car is !!!'

Selective Stencilling

The beauty of many flowers is found both in the delicacy of their shapes and in the distinctive colouration and markings which they bear. Traditional patchwork flowers can often appear solid and stylised.
This is not intended as a a criticism, as this in itself can be a large part of their appeal .... they are simpler, more naive versions of reality. Fine detail cannot be reproduced by piecing alone.
The combination of Paradise Flower designing .... freezer paper piecing .... and selective stencilling offers patchworkers unparalleled creativity.
Gardening catalogues and botanical reference books are great for finding ideas.

Here's how ....

1. Create master and freezer paper duplicate copies as described on p 84.

2. Number all shapes on both.

3. Iron individual shapes to the wrong side of the chosen fabrics, allowing seam allowance space around the individual shapes.
It is essential to use plain fabric for the stencilled design to show clearly.

4. Cut the fabric pieces out individually leaving 1/4 in. seam allowance all around each shape.

5. Stencil shapes individually on the right side of the fabric, before they are sewn together. The paper applied to the wrong side of the fabric does not need to be removed.

6. Do not heat fix the stencil paint until the block has been sewn together...
as excessive ironing may make the freezer paper adhere too firmly to the fabric, making it difficult to remove.

Try the following suggestions................

Selectively stencilling small parts of the design produces effects which are closer to reality. It now becomes possible to colour parts of individual petals ......

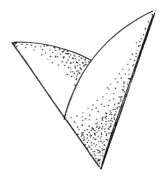

to create diversity between petals on the same flower.

Grade colours in petals and leaves ....
to create the illusion of shadows.

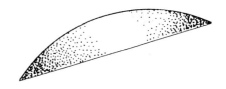

The straight or curved outline of a petal
or leaf can be altered ......
e.g. frilling the edge ...
or adding details impossible to achieve by joining
seams.
A new sophistication becomes possible
... and it is still easy and speedy to achieve.

Add colour around the edges of a shape,
leaving an unpainted centre.
The edges could be an intensified tone of the
fabric colour or one chosen to provide contrast....
or be multi - coloured.

Add colour in one area only........
e.g. the end of the petal which lies towards the centre
of the flower. This could be graded in intensity .....
or change colour as it moves up the petal.

Partially colour a petal by cutting a new paper mask
to create a shape... patterns.... or spots.

Add stamens or tendrils to a flower.

Colour vein effects .... or variegations on leaves.

Well folks! ......
I have shared my ideas in the hope that you will enjoy trying them out .....
and use them to create original items that will become family favourites.
Our experiments today may become the classics of tomorrow ..... and if not ...

who cares ?...... we've had fun!!

By The Same Author........

'Sew Easy Celtic'..... A unique easy way to design your own original Celtic knotwork patterns for needlework and other crafts. Absolutely no artistic or mathematical skill needed for brilliant, fast, machine sewn results. Based on drawing symmetrical doodles .... so anyone can do it ! If you've ever cut out a paper snowflake you can do this!

'Magic Celtic'... More easy designing ... this time using the 'Circle Slice ruler' to draft accurate wedge shaped slices, and more doodles, to create multi - sectional knotwork designs .... they look amazingly complicated... but are easy to draft and fast to machine sew.

'Applique and Roses'..... An applique block and border design technique. This book shows how to easily create limitless original patterns. Fast machine sewing. The same principles can be applied to drafting vine designs also ..... with a new, fast multiple production system for adding 3D roses and leaves.
Forget copying other peoples patterns ... be original ..... create your own in half the time!

'Slice up a Circle'...... easy " geometricks" for patchworkers create wonderful original star, compass, and kaleidoscopic designs. Use the 'Circle Slice ruler' again for easy accuracy. With freezer paper everything fits together like a jig - saw puzzle, and it's easy to add curves without any curved seam piecing.

'Pieceful Scenes"..... gives the traditional blocks of your choice a brand new look by linking them with a landscape in a three dimensional illusion. If you can draw a straight line using a pencil and a ruler you already have all the skills required to draft your own original 3D designs. Freezer paper piecing facilitates fast, trouble free assembly.

The 'Circle Slice Ruler'..... takes all the inaccuracy out of drafting precise angles for multi - sectional designing .... none of the problems of using a protractor !

The ' Multi - Plait' Tool..... another new tool which helps you to draft plaits (braids) quickly and accurately in different styles and sizes. These patterns are suitable for quilting, embroidery, applique or bias applique, for both block and border designs using varying numbers of cords. It is really easy and speedy to use ....
and it takes plaits correctly around corners for you too!

The 'Feather Tool'.... traditional feathered wreathes, borders, hearts, squares etc. are universally popular designs. This tool is the essential aid to fast, original drafting ... feather any shape and in any size for quilting, embroidery, applique and bias applique.

And Lastly ... coming soon .....

Look out for instructions for using Celtic designs and both the above tools to embellish the fronts of store bought sweaters ..... the fast, easy way to create your own designer originals.

If sewing isn't easy, successful and fun ... why do it?